THE
MIDDLE AGES

SARAH HOWARTH

Viking

Acknowledgments

The publishers would like to thank Anne Pearson and Rowena Loverance of the British Museum for their assistance and advice during the preparation of this book; Maureen Pemberton of the Bodleian Library; Michael T. Wright of the Science Museum, Bill Le Fever, who illustrated the see-through pages and cover; and the organizations which have given their permission to reproduce the following pictures:

Ancient Art and Architecture Collection: 15, 27, 29 (bottom), 30 (top right), 36, 44 (bottom)
Leslie Ellison/Ancient Art and Architecture Collection: 6 (bottom)
Bodleian Library, Oxford: 6 (top right), 9, 12, 13, 14, 18 (bottom), 22 (bottom), 26, 28 (top left), 29 (top), 30 (top left), 31, 34, 35, 37, 40 (top and bottom), 44 (top right)
Bridgeman Art Library, London: 39 (bottom)
Eton College, Windsor/Bridgeman Art Library, London: 42 (top)
Louvre, Paris/Giraudon/Bridgeman Art Library, London: 35 (top)
Private Collection/Bridgeman Art Library, London: 32 (top right)
Public Records Office, London/Bridgeman Art Library, London: 22 (top left)
Lukasz Schuster/Wavel State Art Collection, Cracow/Bridgeman Art Library, London: 20
With the kind permission of the Master and Fellows of Corpus Christi College, Cambridge: 23. **e.t. archive:** 8, 10, 11, 16, 19, 21, 32 (top left), 38
Explorer Archives: 6 (top left). **Giraudon:** 44
Michael Holford: 4, 24, 28 (top right)
His Grace the Archbishop of Canterbury and the Trustees of Lambeth Palace Library: 43
R. J. L. Smith, Much Wenlock: 18 (top left)

Illustrators:
Peter Bull: 26. **James Field:** 9, 18-19, 24, 34-35. **Philip Hood:** 10,11, 14, 15, 23, 36-37, 38, 42, 43. **Richard Hook:** 46-47.
Bill Le Fever: Cover, 5, 17, 25, 33, 41. **Nigel Longden:** 4, 12-13, 16, 20, 21, 27, 28, 29.
Kevin Madison: 5. **Shirley Mallinson:** 31. **Maltings Partnership:** 30. **Robert Price:** 32.
Nik Spender (Allied Artists): 7, 45. **Treve Tamblin:** 8, 38-39 (top).

Editor: Julie Good
Series Designer: Nick Leggett
Picture Researchers: Christine Rista and Claire Taylor
Production Controller: Linda Spillane

VIKING
Published by the Penguin Group
Penguin Books USA Inc., 375 Hudson Street, New York, New York 10014, U.S.A.
Penguin Books Ltd, 27 Wrights Lane, London W8 5TZ, England
Penguin Books Australia Ltd, Ringwood, Victoria, Australia
Penguin Books Canada Ltd, 10 Alcorn Avenue, Toronto, Ontario, Canada M4V 3B2
Penguin Books (N.Z.) Ltd, 182–190 Wairau Road, Auckland 10, New Zealand

Penguin Books Ltd, Registered Offices: Harmondsworth, Middlesex, England

First published in Great Britain by Hamlyn Children's Books, 1993

First published in the United States of America by Viking,
a division of Penguin Books USA Inc., 1993

1   3   5   7   9   10   8   6   4   2

Copyright © Reed International Books Ltd. on behalf of Hamlyn Children's Books, 1993
All rights reserved

Library of Congress Catalog Card Number: 92–56930
ISBN 0-670-85098-5
Printed in Belgium by Proost International Book Production
Set in the U.K. by TBC Electronic Publishing

CONTENTS

An Old Power Crumbles 4
A Christian Europe 6
The Family 8
Costume 10
Pastimes 12
Medieval Food 14
Working in the Country 16
Lords and Peasants 18
Becoming a Knight 20
The Life of a Noble 22
Living in a Castle 24
The Crusades 26
Study and Thought 28
Art and Education 30
The Monastic Life 32
Friars and Heresy 34
Towns and Trade 36
Industry 38
Working in the Town 40
Disease and Medicine 42
The Middle Ages End 44
Key Dates and Glossary 46
Index 48

In feudalism, lords swore to obey a king in return for land and power. This scene from the Bayeux Tapestry shows Earl Harold of Wessex taking an oath to Duke William of Normandy.

The Early Middle Ages were times of violence and insecurity. Raids by Germanic tribes had helped to bring the empire of Rome to its knees. Later, in the eighth, ninth, and tenth centuries, there were raids by Vikings, shown here, as well as by Magyars and Saracens.

The period we call the "Middle Ages" stretched roughly from the fifth century A.D. to the fifteenth century. It began with a momentous event: the sack of the great city of Rome and the collapse of the Roman Empire. Although Roman customs continued for a while, a new way of running society, called "feudalism," soon developed. This system, and the increasing power of the Christian Church, were the most important influences on life in the Middle Ages.

THE EMPIRE OF ROME

At the beginning of the first century, the Roman Empire dominated the area from Europe to the north coast of Africa, Palestine, Syria, and Asia Minor. The Roman army first conquered, then policed and mixed with, the many peoples who made up the empire. Roads, towns and cities, forts, and villas spread the Roman way of life. So too did Roman laws and customs, Roman language and education. These things created a wealthy and sophisticated town-based society.

ATTACK!

Raids by Germanic tribes shook the power of the Roman Empire and brought about a new way of life in western Europe. For tribes like the Goths, the Vandals, and the Lombards, war was a normal part of life.

They lived as bands of warriors with chieftains as leaders. The aim of each warrior was to win glory in battle. Their daring raids put the Roman Empire under pressure and disrupted the Roman way of living. Society had to be reorganized, and new ways of maintaining law and order had to be found.

A NEW WAY OF LIFE

One very important change was the custom of strong men offering protection to a band of followers. Powerful individuals, like the Germanic war-chiefs, gave armed protection to their people. In return they expected service—particularly in battle. In the unsettled conditions brought about by the raids of the Germanic tribes and the fall of the Roman Empire, this was very necessary. People were desperate for protection. In Britain, for instance, Roman troops were withdrawn in 442. This left the country exposed to raids by the Saxons, who came from north Germany. A new sort of society was growing up, in which loyalty to an all-powerful local warrior chieftain or "lord" was an important part of life. Each lord ruled a small area, controlling the land and its people by a mixture of loyalty and fear. Historians describe this way of organizing society as "feudalism."

FEUDAL SOCIETY

"Feudal society" is the term used to describe a society in which most people were peasants who lived in poverty and farmed the land. Their time was spent working for a small number of powerful landlords.

The landlords were also military leaders, usually trained as knights, acting as the ruler of the land.

The idea of loyalty and service was very important in feudal society. Anyone who had land took an oath to serve the person who had provided it. For example, lords swore to obey and defend the king or queen who gave them land and power. A special ceremony marked such occasions, so that all would remember it. This was known as an act of homage and fealty. The oath of loyalty was meant to be binding for life and anyone who broke it would be regarded as a traitor.

The map below shows the extent of the Roman Empire at the beginning of the first century A.D.

The map above shows where the various tribes lived in the last years of the Roman Empire. The large map, below, shows the division of countries in about 1100 A.D., when most countries were ruled by kings and queens.

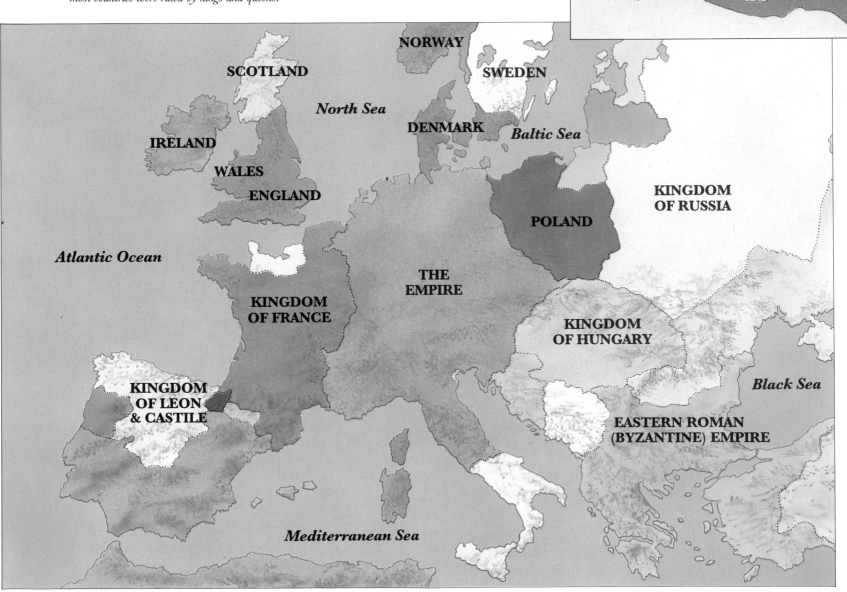

A CHRISTIAN EUROPE

An important change took place in western Europe during the last years of the Roman Empire. In the fourth century, the Emperor Constantine gave up the worship of the old pagan gods of Rome. Instead he began to follow a new religion that had arisen in the east of the empire. It was called Christianity.

The great cathedral of Hagia Sophia was built in the city of Constantinople in the early sixth century. This cathedral, built on the orders of the Eastern Roman Emperor Justinian, dazzled everyone with its beauty.

PAGAN TO CHRISTIAN

The Germanic tribes who attacked the Roman Empire were pagan (they worshipped gods associated with the natural world). Christian missionaries worked in many countries to convert these tribes to Christianity. A monk called Bede, who lived in England in the seventh century, wrote a book about the spread of Christianity. He explained how the missionaries sometimes used pagan customs as a way of helping people understand Christianity. Bede quoted a letter from Pope Gregory I to a missionary named Augustine, who worked among the Anglo-Saxons of England. Gregory told Augustine that he should not destroy pagan temples, but dedicate them to Christ instead.

THE CHURCH OF ROME

As Christianity spread, the Church of Rome developed a very special position. The claim of Rome to be the most important of all Christian churches came to be accepted throughout western Europe. Rome was considered an important religious center by Christians because both St. Peter and St. Paul were believed to have been martyred there. The bishop of Rome (the pope) was regarded as taking the place of St. Peter in the Church. Because of this, he claimed power over Christians everywhere. This claim was disputed in the area that had formed the Roman Empire in the East.

A carved cross erected in Ruthwell in Scotland around the year 700. Many such crosses were erected in Anglo-Saxon times as people were converted to Christianity. Some marked sites where missionaries taught people about the new religion.

A baptism taking place in church. Christian baptism was spread through Europe by missionaries as part of the process of converting different countries to Christianity.

THE POWER OF THE CHURCH

The pope came to have very great power. When the last Roman emperor in the West was thrown from office in 476 A.D., the pope began to play an important part instead. Pope Gregory I (590-604), for example, helped to defend the people of Italy against the Lombard raiders who had attacked them. He also carried out many tasks that had previously been the work of the emperor's officials, such as distributing corn. The actions of popes like Gregory I meant that the Church came to have political as well as religious power.

The pope and other leading members of the clergy claimed the right to influence many aspects of government in different countries. They believed that the authority of kings and queens was given to them by the Church. The coronation ceremony was a sign of this belief. When a king or queen was crowned, it was an important clergyman, such as an archbishop, who placed the crown on the new ruler's head. The pope himself crowned the Emperor Charlemagne in 800. Many believed that rituals like this showed that the Church was more powerful and important than kings and queens.

THE WEALTH OF THE CHURCH

The power and wealth of the Church were obvious to many people in their everyday lives. The buildings of the Church made everyone aware of these things. Few villages were without a church—a stone building which towered above the little huts and cottages of the peasants. In many places there were also large monasteries and cathedrals, magnificent complexes of buildings designed in the most up-to-date architectural styles. They were elaborate and costly to build. Many medieval church buildings may still be seen, such as the Abbaye-aux-Hommes in Caen, Normandy, and Speyer Cathedral in Germany. These buildings dedicated to God dominated the landscape and made private houses look small and insignificant. Only the castles of high-ranking nobles and knights made an impression like this.

A PART OF EVERYDAY LIFE

Religious belief was a part of everyday life in the Middle Ages, which also contributed to the power of the Church. People looked to the Church and its leaders to explain events in the world around them. Disasters like storms, disease, or famine were often explained as punishments sent by God. People hoped that prayer and religious devotion would keep away events of this kind.

When the people of Europe were first converted to Christianity, many pagan places of worship were taken over and used for Christian services. In time, fine buildings were specially built for Christian worship. Here we see a great cathedral being built.

THE FAMILY

In the Middle Ages it was very unusual for people to choose what sort of work they did, whom they married, or how they were educated. These things depended on the sort of family each person belonged to, and they were very difficult to change. Poor peasant families had a very different way of life from the families of knights, noblemen, or townspeople.

GROWING UP

Babies were baptized soon after birth since many died of disease in the first days of life. The ceremony of baptism made the child a member of the Church. Children were treated strictly. From about the age of ten children were expected to take part in adult life. Children in poor families worked to help provide for the family. Children of nobles were often brought up by other families to improve relations between the families. Boys were taught how to fight on horseback and how knights should behave. Girls were taught how to look after a large household.

The members of a peasant family in their cottage. Peasants often worked long and hard and their houses, clothes, and possessions were plain and practical.

This picture shows a wedding ceremony in progress. Marriage was important in the Middle Ages because it was looked on as a way to bring two families together. It was especially important for wealthy and powerful people.

SURNAMES

The surnames of wealthy families were often taken from the name of the most important part of their lands. In poorer families, surnames were taken from trades, such as "Tailor" or "Smith," or from the place in which the family lived. Sometimes people were known simply as someone's son or daughter—"Jack's son," for example.

WOMEN

Medieval women had little power over their lives. Many peasant women had to work for the lord on his estates. It was the custom for him to decide when the women on his land would marry, and to allow them to take a husband only from men who lived on the manor. The lord sometimes allowed a woman to marry someone from another manor in return for a payment in money or goods.

Few women were given an education, although girls in the families of well-to-do knights were sometimes taught to read. We know of some exceptions to this rule. One was a woman named Heloise, who lived in France in the twelfth century. She was brought up by her uncle, a clergyman. He was proud of her, and had her well educated.

WEALTHY HOUSEHOLDS

The homes of wealthy knights were always full of people. Many people were keen to enter the service of especially powerful families. It was considered an honor to be allowed to do so. For some, it was also a way of winning riches. The men who served important nobles as faithful servants, for example, might receive suits of clothes, valuable war-horses, or other gifts.

Households like these included many other people. There would be jesters, entertainers, and travelers on long journeys who had stopped to ask for hospitality. You could also find servants—cooks to work in the kitchens, men to work in the stables, falconers to train and look after the birds of prey used for hunting, and many others.

The lord, lady, and a friend relaxing in his castle. There was little privacy in the castle. Whether eating, sleeping, settling down for a quiet minute, sewing, or talking, other people were never far away.

At the age of seven, the boy's father gave him into the care of another . . . He learned to ride with shield and lance. He learned to make a horse gallop and spent many hours fencing, wrestling, jumping, throwing the javelin, and hunting.

— Gottfried von Strassburg —

POOR HOUSEHOLDS

The households of the poor were very different. Here there was room only for a small number of people, because peasants had to make sure they could provide enough food to feed their family. There were many difficulties, and for many poor families providing food was a great problem. When peasants wanted to get married, they had to decide if they had enough land to support a family. All members of the family would sleep in the same room at night.

A king and his family. Compare the clothes worn by these people with those of the peasant family on the opposite page. Evidence of this kind shows the very different ways of life led by different groups of people in medieval society.

9

COSTUME

This shield shows the coat of arms of an important family from Florence. Only rich and powerful people had the right to a coat of arms, which was a sign of status.

In the Middle Ages the clothes a person wore were a clear sign of his or her position in society. Peasants dressed very simply, while wealthy townspeople dressed more splendidly. The clothes of noblemen and noblewomen used the finest materials and jewels.

CLOTHES FOR THE POOR

The poor made their own clothes by spinning and weaving cloth at home. Men wore tunics that reached to mid-thigh, and a pair of hose or leggings. They also wore a hood called a "capuchon." It went over the shoulders and had a long pointed end called a "liripipe." This could be wrapped around and around for extra warmth, like a scarf. Women wore a long tunic, and children dressed in clothes much like their parents.

CLOTHES FOR THE RICH

For the poor, styles changed very little. For the knights and nobility it was different. One chronicler from Normandy, a part of modern France, noticed how fashions changed when the Normans conquered England in 1066. He said that the Anglo-Saxons were influenced by new fashions from Europe. One very obvious influence was the very closely cropped hairstyle of the Norman men. This can be seen on the Bayeux Tapestry, which tells the story of the Normans' victory.

In countries across Europe, the costume of the wealthy was very splendid. They used expensive materials, such as silks and velvets. Men and women wore mantles or cloaks, and their outer robes were often slashed open to reveal the contrasting garment beneath.

CLOTHES AND SOCIAL STANDING

A story written in the ninth century about the Emperor Charlemagne shows the importance of costume in medieval society. It was written by his chaplain, a man named Einhard. He described how Charlemagne's courtiers had visited Italy to buy magnificent clothing trimmed with peacock feathers, pheasant skin, silks, ribbons, and ermine (fur). Dressed in their new clothes, they went to the emperor's court. Charlemagne was displeased at their show of finery. On this particular occasion he had dressed very simply. To teach his courtiers a lesson, he gave instructions that they should immediately go out hunting, without stopping to change their clothes. The nobles' fine clothes were torn to pieces in the forest, but Charlemagne's were not. In this way Charlemagne pointed out that it was unwise for the nobles to dress more grandly than the emperor!

Spinning thread and carding wool to make cloth. Clothing was made by hand in the Middle Ages, and tasks like these were regarded as women's work. Even today, unmarried women are sometimes called "spinsters," the name given to women who spun thread.

Monks—like those shown here—and nuns dressed very simply in order to show that their thoughts were set on God. They wore long woolen robes in plain colors.

Laws were sometimes passed to stop poorer people from wearing the sort of clothing that was usually worn by the nobility. These are known as "sumptuary laws." Laws like these were made in England in 1463. They ordered that "common laborers" were not to wear cloth that cost more than two shillings per yard. Only nobles were supposed to dress in bright colors like scarlet, blue, and green.

CLOTHES AND WORK

The dress of medieval people not only made a statement about how much wealth or power they had. It also told others about their work. Monks and nuns, for instance, wore habits to tell people which monastic community they belonged to. The Cistercians wore white habits, made of plain, undyed cloth. They were known as "White" monks. Benedictines wore black habits and were known as "Black" monks. Other people often dressed to show either their work or religious beliefs.

CLOTHES AND SYMBOLISM

Many people wore a special costume when they went on a pilgrimage to pray at the shrine of a famous saint. The pilgrim's costume was a simple robe made of wool. Sometimes he or she would carry a long staff with a hook on the end. Many went barefoot. On the return journey pilgrim badges were often sewn on to their clothing. These badges were bought at the pilgrimage center, and showed which shrine the pilgrim had visited. Pilgrims to Jerusalem wore a cross on their robe, and returned with a piece of palm as their badge.

The servants and knights of great nobles frequently wore clothing that showed whom they supported. They wore robes displaying their lord or lady's coat of arms or heraldic badge.

A lord and lady with musicians and a servant. The life-style of important nobles and their families was grand and full of ceremony.

11

For many people there was little distinction between work and leisure time. Many pastimes served a dual purpose: they were not only entertainment but also provided food for the table or improved military skills.

A king being amused by the court fool or jester. Some jesters were given valuable gifts for particularly entertaining performances.

A tournament with two knights competing. Tournaments became very popular in the Middle Ages, but the Church disapproved of them.

PASTIMES OF THE POOR

The pastimes of the poorest peasants reflected their agricultural way of life. At harvest time, the lord of the manor provided great feasts to encourage and reward his laborers. More celebrations followed once the grain was safely stored. Trials of strength were often held. Some involved lifting as much grass or straw as possible on the handle of a sickle. Pigs, straw, and timber were awarded as prizes.

Poaching, though illegal, was another common sporting pastime for the poor. Many peasants hunted rabbits, deer, and birds—even the smallest birds would end up on the table.

VILLAGE LIFE

Games and dancing played an important part in village life. Sports like soccer, wrestling, and hockey were played in many parts of Europe. They were rougher versions of the modern sports, played with far fewer rules. Dances, with pipe and fiddle accompaniment, were often held in churchyards, and on May Day there were special customs to be observed, including dances around a maypole set up in the village.

TOURNAMENTS

Tournaments and hunting formed the favorite pastimes of the knights and nobility. Like the pastimes of the poor, these activities were not meant only for pleasure: they also had a serious purpose, training men in the skills of warfare.

The first tournaments were battles staged between rival groups of knights. These became very popular, and in the twelfth century, knights would travel great distances

across Europe to fight when they heard that a tournament was to be held. Those on the winning side won rich prizes: valuable war-horses, armor, and rewards of money. And, just as important, they might attract the attention of a wealthy nobleman who would take them into his service, giving them an opportunity to win more riches. Many were killed in these early tournaments. Over sixty knights died in one tournament held near Cologne! Later, tournaments became less violent, centering on the joust, a competition between two mounted knights. These occasions were colorful and festive spectacles, attracting great crowds of spectators.

HOLY DAYS

The modern word "holiday" originally meant "holy day"—a saint's day, on which work stopped. Special celebrations marked such days. There were processions on the feast of Corpus Christi (to show devotion to Jesus Christ), and feasts and mummers' plays (plays performed by masked actors) during the twelve days of Christmas. Saints' days were often chosen as days on which fairs were held.

At the fair there were many different sorts of entertainment. These ranged from troubadours (traveling minstrels) to jugglers, acrobats, and peddlers. Many of the celebrations associated with these holy days had their roots in pagan customs. For example, the lighting of bonfires on the eve of the feast of St. John the Baptist, June 23, corresponds to the pagan celebration of the summer solstice.

Scenes like this took place when traveling performers like jugglers, acrobats, and musicians visited towns and villages.

A nobleman out hunting on horseback carrying a falcon on his wrist. Medieval noblemen and noblewomen often spent large sums of money buying and training birds like these. The birds would be let loose to hunt smaller birds and animals.

HOW DO WE KNOW ?

Historians study many kinds of evidence to learn about medieval pastimes. Some of the evidence is written down. The accounts drawn up for kings and the nobility, for instance, sometimes show payments for hawks, hunting dogs, and to entertainers and minstrels. Medieval art also provides details about how people spent their leisure: people played chess and board games like back-gammon, as well as games like blind-man's buff.

MEDIEVAL FOOD

The diet of medieval people was very different from ours today. Most country people grew their own food, and were sometimes in danger of starvation. The diet of the wealthy was more varied. Feasts were an important part of people's social life.

This picture shows medieval kitchen equipment. Meat was roasted on a spit, and pots were hung over the fire to boil meat, vegetables, and other foods.

The kitchen of a great castle. By modern standards it was probably none too clean, had its share of bad smells, and was a hot and noisy place to work.

WHAT DID THEY EAT?

Archaeologists can provide us with evidence about health and diet in the Middle Ages, and some recipe books survive from this time. Paintings, letters, and written accounts also tell us about the period.

Medieval people used many strongly flavored herbs and spices in their cooking, partly to help disguise the taste of food that was going bad. These included pepper, saffron, cinnamon, and cumin. Such spices were brought to Europe by merchants from the East and were very expensive. There were few easy ways of preserving food, so it was always possible that meat or dairy foods would grow moldy. Wine often went bad, and so was sometimes served with spices like ginger or with honey.

Pudding of Porpoise:
Take the blood of the porpoise and the fat, and oatmeal, salt, pepper, and ginger and mix these well and put these in the gut of the porpoise. Then let the porpoise cook, and serve it.

Fifteenth-century recipe

Many different animals were hunted for food. A medieval banquet for the wealthy might include delicacies such as swan, heron, peacock, whale, porpoise, or small birds.

Peasants had much less variety in their diet. For them, many meals consisted of cabbage, leeks, onions, or other vegetables, oatmeal porridge, and dark bread.

FOOD AND FAMINE

Peasants had to grow their own food. Many also had to provide food for the lord of the manor on whose land they lived. This was a sort of rent, paid in goods rather than money. Peasant farmers had many problems growing enough food. The winter was a particularly hard time and their supplies sometimes ran out. An English poet named William Langland described the conditions in which peasants lived. His account explained how they tried to survive through the winter on bread made out of beans and oats, vegetables, and, occasionally, on an egg and some cheese.

Sometimes there was famine. At the start of the fourteenth century there was severe weather, and a series of bad harvests followed. Outbreaks of disease among sheep and cattle took place and the living conditions for many poor people became very bad. Resistance to illness was lowered, and many died from lack of food and from disease.

FEASTS

Feasting was an important part of medieval life. Feasts were given to reward the peasants who worked to get in the harvest each year.

A pestle and mortar. The pestle was used to mash ingredients inside the mortar to prepare them for cooking. All wealthy medieval households would have needed a pestle and mortar in the kitchen.

Sometimes the lord of the manor also provided a meal for the workers at other times. This might be bread and ale, or a dish of meat and peas. Great feasts were also a regular part of the life of the castle. Here, elaborate ceremonies were an important feature. It was a common custom for a trumpeter to play to announce the start of the meal. The guests were given places at table according to their social importance. They were served in pairs, with food for each couple set down in one dish and shared.

FOOD AND FAITH

Monks and nuns tried to eat a very simple diet and give up rich foods as a sign that they were not interested in everyday matters. A famous Cistercian monk named Bernard of Clairvaux, living in France in the twelfth century, wrote a letter describing the foods he thought monks should live on. These were vegetables, beans, bread, and water.

Medieval people sometimes changed their diet for religious reasons. They occasionally went without food, fasting as a mark of devotion to God. The Catholic Church directed that everyone should give up meat on Fridays as a religious gesture. Many people ate fish instead.

A banquet at the castle. The lord and lady of the castle sat at the top table with important guests.

This picture shows a page from the Domesday Book. *The book is a record of land in England, made for King William I in 1086. It shows how the countryside was farmed at this time.*

Peasants like these not only had to farm the land to provide their own food, they also had to give some of their crops to the lord of the manor.

Most people who worked in the country were involved in agriculture. Most farming was carried out on a small scale. But, as time went by, some people began to farm for profit, rather than simply to provide their own food.

AGRICULTURE

In the Middle Ages many people were needed to farm the land. They raised crops and looked after livestock. Peasants had small strips of land to grow food. Many kept a few chickens, too, with perhaps a sheep or cow. On the lands belonging to the lord of the manor, crops like barley and wheat were grown. When harvested, they were taken to the mill to be ground into flour for bread. Sheep were raised for wool, cows for milk, and pigs for their meat.

In the thirteenth century important developments in farming took place. More specialized crops were grown. Grapes were grown in France, rice in Lombardy, and hops on the Rhine in Germany.

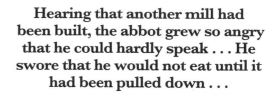

Hearing that another mill had been built, the abbot grew so angry that he could hardly speak . . . He swore that he would not eat until it had been pulled down . . .

—— Jocelin of Brakelond ——

THE MILLER

The miller was often one of the most prosperous people in the village. Villagers had to pay the miller to use his mill. The payment was usually in kind—the miller would be entitled to keep a certain amount of the corn. Many millers had a reputation for dishonesty, and were accused of taking more corn than they should.

MILL TOLLS

In many places the mill was owned by the lord of the manor. The peasants who lived on his land were obliged to grind their corn at his mill. Like the miller, the lord was entitled to part of the corn. This mill toll formed an important part of the lord's income. For this reason the lord was always concerned that no other mills should be built on his land without his permission.

POWER AND INDUSTRY

Water mills harnessed water power. Windmills were also built during the Middle Ages and these employed wind power. Both were used mainly to mill corn, but in time water mills were put to a number of different uses. Some were used to make paper. The first German paper mill was erected toward the end of the fourteenth century. Some water mills were used to help in the process of clothmaking, and were known as fulling mills.

The first fulling mills in England were recorded at the end of the twelfth century, becoming more widespread by the fourteenth century. Developments like these that harnessed water power began to bring industry into parts of the countryside where there were plenty of swiftly moving rivers.

WATER POWER

1 Overshot wheel
2 Miller
3 Roof timbers
4 Hopper
5 Wooden casing
6 Millstones
7 Pit wheel
8 Grain bin
9 Thatched roof

Millstones

Water mills

Before water mills were introduced, corn was
ground with hand mills known as "querns."
From the tenth century on, water mills were
built in many parts of Europe. When corn
was brought for grinding, it was hoisted to the
top of the mill. From here it was gradually
poured from a hopper down to a pair of great
round millstones. The millstones turned and
crushed the corn, grinding it into flour. Water
mills at this time generally used a waterwheel
called an "overshot" wheel. To work this type
of wheel, water was channeled toward the
mill so that it tumbled on to the very top of
the wheel. The force of the water turned the
wheel and operated the machinery.

LORDS AND PEASANTS

During the Middle Ages the countryside was divided into large estates dominated by powerful lords. The lord's lands were farmed for him by the peasants who lived on them.

A scene showing grapes being harvested. Agricultural work like this was usually carried out by peasants as part of the labor services they owed to the lord of the manor.

POWERFUL LORDS

In the unsettled centuries at the beginning of the Middle Ages, after the fall of the Roman Empire in the West, men who could offer protection and leadership to their neighbors were given many powers. The title that people at the time used to describe powerful men like these was "dominus," a Latin word meaning "lord" or "master."

Sometimes these strong men seized land and power for themselves. One man who was well-known for acting in this way was Fulk Nerra, Count of Anjou (now in modern France), who lived in the early eleventh century. Later it became the custom for the king or queen to grant land to powerful men on the condition that they provided military support to the king when it was needed.

Each lord ruled over his estates. The money and produce of the estates made some lords very wealthy, and they enjoyed a very good standard of life compared with the peasants who served them.

Here soldiers take produce from a group of villagers. This often happened in times of war, when villages were reduced to poverty in order to feed bands of soldiers passing by. Many French villages suffered in this way during the Hundred Years War.

A medieval picture of bees swarming around the hives. Sugar played no part in medieval recipes. To make food taste sweet, honey was used. Beekeeping was therefore very important in the Middle Ages.

GREAT ESTATES

Each estate aimed to be self-sufficient. In the ninth century, the Emperor Charlemagne ordered that all his estates should have a blacksmith, shoemakers, soap-makers, bakers, and many other different craftsmen.

Estates at this time were divided into small areas called "manors." These were run for the lord by officials such as the "reeve" and "bailiff," who controlled the work done on the estate and prepared accounts. Each estate had its own customs, which regulated the relationship between the lord and his tenants (the people who lived on his land). These were not written down at first: they were re-membered and handed on by word of mouth.

FREE AND UNFREE

Medieval law divided the peasants into two groups: those who were free and those who were unfree. Unfree peasants were sometimes known as "villeins" or "serfs." Villeins were unfree because they had to obey their lord completely. They had to work on his land, and were not allowed to move away. The land that villeins farmed, and all their animals, belonged to the lord. When a villein died, the best animal had to be given to the lord. This custom was called "heriot."

A villein could become free by buying freedom from the lord, or by becoming a priest. Villeins who ran away to a town might become free—or they might be caught and severely punished. In the fourteenth century many villeins grew discontented with this way of life. A revolt broke out in England in 1381. This was called the "Peasants' Revolt." The peasants were quickly defeated.

WORKERS

The lord needed people to work on his estates. This was the peasants' main duty. In time records were made that noted what work was expected. This included tasks like plowing, harrowing, mowing hay, getting in the harvest, washing sheep, and carting goods from one part of the estate to another. Such duties were known as "labor services." They varied from place to place. Records from one German monastery in a vine-growing area in the fifteenth century described how the peasants living on the monastery's lands had to carry wine-casks from the vineyards to the monastery as part of their labor services.

In the thirteenth century many lords made great efforts to run their estates profitably, and books of instruction were drawn up to help them. One famous book was Walter of Henley's *Hosebondrie*. Books like this described the people who worked on great estates, such as plowmen and dairymaids, and the work they had to do.

A peasant cutting corn. Medieval farming was very labor-intensive, requiring many people to work the land and get in the harvest. Today, machinery takes the place of workers.

The sword played an important part in the ceremony when a man became a knight.

An experienced knight confers knighthood on a young man, giving him a blow on the neck with the flat of a sword.

Knights had a high position in medieval society. Because conditions were often violent and unsettled, military power was very important. The knights were a warrior elite, and their status in society reflected this importance.

A WARRIOR ELITE

Knights fought on horseback as cavalry troops. The cavalry were the most important troops in medieval armies. Their armor, equipment, and war-horses were very expensive, and few people could afford them. At great fairs in Champagne in the thirteenth century, for example, war-horses were sold for about $130 each. It would take an ordinary foot soldier 32 years to earn that amount of money.

A knight and crossbowman. Knights fought on horseback, and the rest of the medieval army was made up of soldiers who fought on foot.

BECOMING A KNIGHT

The sons of knights were sent to the household of another knight at about the age of twelve to learn the skills of knighthood. They were trained by serving the knight in many ways—by grooming his horses and looking after his armor, for example. A young man who served a knight in this way was called a "squire." Squires also learned to ride and fight on horseback, and to look after weapons. One skill considered particularly important was serving the lord with food at table.

By the thirteenth century complicated ceremonies had developed to mark the occasion on which a man finally became a knight. On the day before the ceremony, the knight-to-be took a special bath, and then dressed in white clothes. He spent the night in prayer in church, kneeling in front of the altar on which his sword and armor lay. Early the next morning Mass was said in church, then the knight was dressed in his armor. Prayers were said over the armor and sword. These were intended to dedicate the knight and his work to God. Finally another knight dealt him a blow on the neck with his hand or sword. The new knight vowed to act according to the code of chivalry.

A knight on horseback. Learning to ride and fight on horseback were vital parts of the knight's training. Boys learning the skills of knighthood had to become good at grooming and looking after their horses.

THE CODE OF CHIVALRY

The word "chivalry" comes from the French word for knight, *chevalier*. A famous bishop who lived in France in the twelfth century wrote a list of the qualities he thought a knight should have. These included respect for the Church, pity for the poor, and bravery. Qualities like these summed up the ideals of chivalry. Knights vowed to behave with courtesy, especially toward women, and were expected to keep their word. They swore to serve the lord who knighted them.

Evidence about the code of chivalry is found in many poems and legends composed at this time. Among the most famous are the tales of the knights of King Arthur written by a man named Chrétien de Troyes who lived in France in the twelfth century. He wrote about the legends that grew up around King Arthur and his court.

WEAPONS

The knights' chief weapons were a sword and a lance, a kind of spear that measured up to fifteen feet long. The knight could throw the lance at his enemy, or charge at his opponent and try to unseat him from his horse. Swords were highly valued, and they were often set with jewels. Sometimes relics (sacred remains of a holy person) were set inside the pommel, near the handle of the sword. Battle-axes and maces were also used.

ARMOR

Armor was worn as protection. It changed over time to keep pace with changes in weapons and developments in the way battles were fought. In the eleventh century armor was made of mail (metal rings linked together). From the fourteenth century, plate armor became more common because it offered better protection.

A young man called a squire helped the knight put on his armor for battle. Armor was essential for the protection of the knight, and dressing could take as long as an hour to complete.

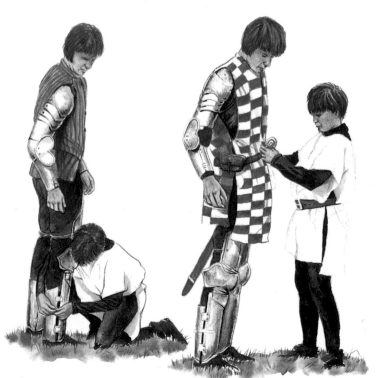

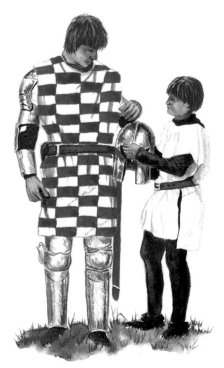

THE LIFE OF A NOBLE

The seal of King Edward IV of England. Knights and nobles often used seals like this. They carried symbols from the coat of arms, or other signs to identify the person using the seal, to leave a wax impression on important documents.

Noblewomen like these were brought up to command large households. They had to oversee the cooks and servants, and help nurse those who were ill. In time of war they might have to help defend the castle.

In the Middle Ages the nobility had great powers. They were the most important group in society. Many nobles were wealthy, and led lives of considerable luxury. But the Middle Ages was also a time of lawlessness and violence when many wars were fought.

POWER AND WEALTH

It was very difficult for kings and queens to rule without the support of their nobles. There were two important reasons for this. Firstly, they needed a force of fighting men to call on if their power was threatened. Secondly, because there were few roads and travel was difficult, it was hard for a ruler to make his or her power felt in distant parts of the kingdom.

The king arranged his journeys very carefully, and gave everyone notice of the days on which he would travel, with the number of days and names of the villages in which he would stay.

Walter Map

It was unusual for even the wealthiest nobles to be able to read or write during the Middle Ages, so they were sometimes entertained by poets and other writers reading aloud from their work.

FIEFS AND SERVICE

Rulers gave large estates all over the kingdom to their vassals (supporters). People at the time described these estates as "fiefs." When a man was given a fief, he received much power over the people who lived on it. But he also had to make special promises in return. He had to support the ruler and come to fight, bringing his own supporters, when the ruler needed him. The ruler told his vassals how many soldiers they must provide, and insisted that they were only to bring knights—the best soldiers of the time.

A LIFE OF TRAVEL

Because many lords had fiefs scattered over a large area, much of their time was spent traveling from one fief to another. These journeys were undertaken to make sure that the people who lived on their land were loyal to them. The journeys also had another, very practical, purpose—the nobles stayed at each part of their estates for long enough to consume the stores of food each estate had produced! Even the king led a life of travel like this. One writer who lived in the twelfth century, named Walter Map, described how King Henry I of England traveled around his kingdom, and the organization that this involved. The arrangements were made well in advance, and the whole household, with horses and hounds, official documents, tapestries, carpets, and tableware, was packed up and moved on.

A LIFE OF WARFARE

Noblemen fought as knights. Much of their time was spent in activities like hunting, or fighting in tournaments that were good practice for war. War brought wealth to many noblemen. In the Hundred Years War, fought between England and France, ransoms and lands taken from the French brought wealth to many English noblemen.

The nobles also acted as advisers to kings and queens. But disagreements broke out, sometimes leading to armed rebellion. This happened in many places. In England in the fourteenth century the Earl of Lancaster challenged King Edward II. His supporters fought the king and were defeated.

The noble and his family lived in a castle. Many medieval castles survive as ruins, including Krak des Chevaliers in Syria, Chateau Gaillard in France, and Chepstow in Wales. Castles were military strongholds designed to give maximum security. Only in the fourteenth century did the nobility begin to build homes that were designed for a more peaceful way of life.

A LIFE OF LUXURY

Many nobles were wealthy, and their lives were luxurious by medieval standards. They were among the few people who slept on a wooden bed with a mattress, silk or linen sheets, fur coverings, and curtains to give privacy. From the thirteenth century the wealthiest nobles sometimes had glass in the windows of their castles.

Elaborate wall-hangings provided decoration and kept out drafts. Castles often had paintings on the walls. King Henry III of England, who lived in the thirteenth century, was especially fond of paintings like these. The use of tapestry coverings for the floor spread from places like Spain to other countries in the fourteenth century.

Hunting was one of the most popular pastimes for nobles. In this illustration a deer is chased by riders with great hounds.

23

In the living quarters of the castle, walls were often hung with tapestries like this. They provided decoration and also had a practical purpose—they made the room a little warmer.

A motte and bailey castle. This was one of the earliest types of castle built in Europe.

Castles were first built in Europe in the ninth and tenth centuries. Their owners ruled the surrounding area, and built castles to offer strength and safety to everyone who lived in them. Their design changed over time to keep up with developments in the way wars were fought.

LIVING CONDITIONS

Castles were built to guard the interests of the king or lord, and also served as a home for the lord's servants, soldiers, and knights, as well as his family. They were very expensive to build and maintain.

Many medieval castles can still be seen today. These buildings tell us a lot about the ordinary life of the people who lived in them. Castel del Monte in Italy, for example, was planned to provide the most up-to-date and luxurious setting for Emperor Frederick II and his court. The floors were decorated with colorful mosaics and, thanks to techniques learned from the Arabs, there were even flushing lavatories! At this time sophisticated arrangements of this sort were very unusual. Most castle interiors were very basic, with straw and rushes on the floors to keep out the cold.

THE CASTLE UNDER SIEGE

A number of special machines were used to lay siege to castles. These included the "mangon" and the "trebuchet." Siege engines like these were loaded with stones which were then hurled at the castle walls. The aim was to make a large hole in the walls and force an entry.

DIFFERENT WAYS TO BUILD

Many ways to build castles were tried over the centuries. One type of castle, called the motte and bailey, was useful for an invading army because it could be built quickly, out of earth and wood. When the Normans settled in the British Isles, they built many such castles. Stone was later used to build motte and bailey and other types of castles.

There were also experiments with the shape of the castle's towers. At first, towers were rectangular in shape. They were fairly easy for an enemy to attack, and so round ones were built instead. It was harder for the enemy to force out stones and bring them crashing to the ground, since the stones radiated out from a central point. Changes in design like these gave better protection to the people who lived inside the castle.

THE CASTLE

Who lived in a castle?

The castle was the home of a nobleman and his family. But the household also contained many more people—soldiers, servants, retainers, and children from other noble families who were being brought up and trained there. The lord of the castle ruled over all its inhabitants, including his family. He would often be away from home, and during this time his wife, the lady of the castle, took control. If the castle was attacked, she organized the defense. Sometimes noblewomen led the defense in person.

Siege extension

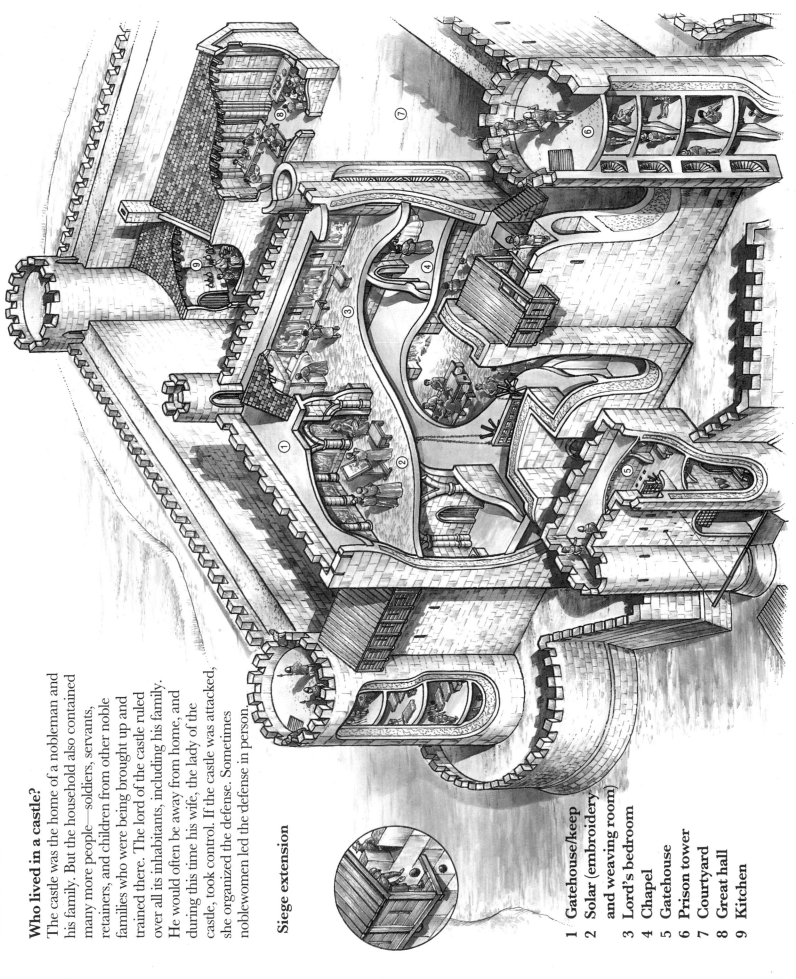

1 Gatehouse/keep
2 Solar (embroidery and weaving room)
3 Lord's bedroom
4 Chapel
5 Gatehouse
6 Prison tower
7 Courtyard
8 Great hall
9 Kitchen

THE CRUSADES

A scene from the Crusades. The Crusades were wars fought with great savageness. The Crusaders attacked Muslims, Jews, and other groups.

This map shows the routes taken by important knights leading the Crusaders to the Holy Land.

The Crusades were holy wars fought by Europeans believing they were upholding the Christian religion against the invasion of the Islamic religion. Many Crusades were waged between the eleventh and thirteenth centuries, but only the First Crusade really succeeded in its aims.

THE HOLY LAND
Medieval Christians greatly respected the lands of Palestine described in the Old and New Testaments. For many believers, a visit to this "Holy Land" to pray and worship was a lifetime's ambition.

Many did not believe that people of different religions could live peacefully together. The Catholic Church taught that Christianity was the only true religion. It aimed to convert those with different beliefs, like the Jews and Muslims.

Jerusalem itself had been ruled by Muslims from the seventh century. At first, relations between Christian pilgrims and the Muslims had been peaceful. Muslim traders provided food, transport, and other necessities for the pilgrims. The income that this exchange provided was useful to the local economy.

1096	FIRST CRUSADE
1147	SECOND CRUSADE
1189	THIRD CRUSADE
1204	FOURTH CRUSADE
1212	CHILDREN'S CRUSADE

This table shows when some of the most important Crusades took place. The Crusades attracted many different sorts of people, including peasants, and were not the well-disciplined fighting force hoped for.

In the eleventh century the relationship began to change. The Fatimid Caliphs of Egypt were thrown from power by the Seljuk Turks. These new rulers were much more aggressive, and Christian pilgrimage became a dangerous affair.

Make this journey and your sins will be forgiven.

Pope Urban II

A CALL FOR HELP
The increase in Seljuk power was viewed with alarm in western Europe. Developments at Jerusalem and in the Byzantine Empire (the Eastern Roman Empire) were especially worrying. Then, in 1095, the Byzantine emperor, Alexius Comnenus, wrote to the pope, desperately asking for help against the Turks.

A great Church council had been called to meet in Clermont in France late in the year 1095 by Pope Urban II. He explained that Christian holy places were in Turkish hands, and called on Christian believers to rescue the Holy Land. Those listening were told that the Crusade was God's will, and that if they died in the struggle their sins would be forgiven. The response was immediate. Crying "Deus vult," the Latin for "God wills it," many in the congregation vowed at once that they would set out on Crusade for the Holy Land.

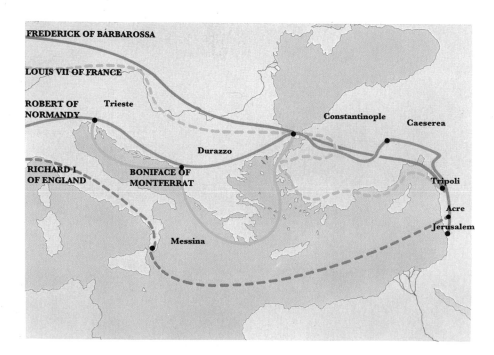

FREDERICK OF BÁRBAROSSA

LOUIS VII OF FRANCE

ROBERT OF NORMANDY Trieste

RICHARD I OF ENGLAND BONIFACE OF MONTFERRAT

Durazzo

Constantinople Caeserea

Tripoli

Acre

Jerusalem

Messina

ON CRUSADE

Many different sorts of people answered the call to go on Crusade. The First Crusade attracted a large number of poor people who were led by a man from France named Peter the Hermit. In 1212 many children from France and Germany set out on Crusade, and in 1251 many shepherds left Europe for the Holy Land. All hoped to win back Jerusalem from the Muslims.

Fighting forces of knights also went on Crusade. The leaders of such bands included important noblemen and princes, such as Baldwin of Flanders, who fought in the First Crusade, and the Emperor Frederick Barbarossa from Germany, who was one of the leaders of the Third Crusade in 1189. King Richard I of England was a keen Crusader. He took part in the Third Crusade, and fought the Saracen leader, Saladin. He won an important battle at Jaffa, before being captured and held for ransom in Germany on his way back to England.

Richard I of England, with the red and gold shield, one of the leaders of the Third Crusade, fights the Saracen leader, Saladin. Saladin suggested that the two sides should make peace, and that Richard should marry Saladin's sister to seal the treaty. Christians were horrified at the idea.

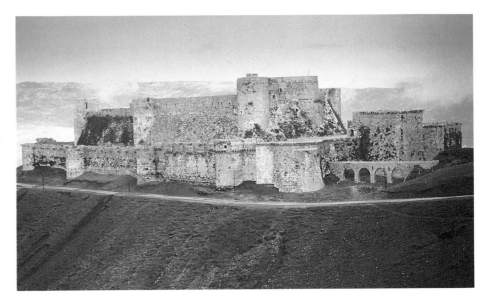

VIOLENCE AND CANNIBALISM

The Crusades were marked by much violence and cruelty. Many Muslims were massacred, for example when the Crusaders took the city of Jerusalem in 1099. It was not only the Muslims who suffered. Attacks were also made on communities of Jewish people living in countries like France and Germany. These attacks were carried out by armies on their way to the Crusades.

Conditions for soldiers in the Holy Land were harsh. The Crusaders had little knowledge of the climate and conditions there, and many were ill-prepared for their campaigns. During the First Crusade supplies of food ran short. Stories written by eyewitnesses describe how the Crusaders ate dogs, rats, and even human bodies.

The castle of Krak des Chevaliers, built by the Crusader Knights of St. John in Syria. Castles of this type had a number of rings of fortifications.

This is a page from a "bestiary"—a book written about animals. In books like this, medieval scholars aimed to write down everything that was known about a particular subject, collecting all sorts of facts and legends.

Many monasteries were centers of learning, and most of the beautifully illustrated books were crafted by the monks.

During the Middle Ages the Christian Church in western Europe played a dominant part in forming people's ideas about the world. It taught that knowledge was important as a way of finding out about God.

KNOWLEDGE AND RELIGION

In the medieval period the study of the Bible was thought to be more important than any other kind of knowledge. In the fifth century St. Augustine, a great Christian thinker, said that people could study music, numbers, plants, animals, precious stones, and other subjects—but only because these subjects would help them to understand the Bible better. Many people shared his views. For them, the study of secular subjects (subjects concerned with the world, rather than God) took second place to religion.

The way people looked at the world was greatly affected by their religious belief. Many believed that everyone—and everything—in the universe had a special task to do, and that this task was given by God. The sun had to give light, the king had to rule, and the peasant had to grow food.

An astrolabe made by a German craftsman. The astrolabe was an instrument used to help sailors navigate their ships. Many medieval scholars were interested in the astrolabe, including the English poet Chaucer.

BUILDING ON THE PAST

The learning of ancient Greek writers was greatly respected, and some Christian scholars tried to make the works of the ancient Greeks more widely known in the Christian West. An Italian named Boethius was important in this process. He translated Greek works, such as those of Aristotle, into Latin. Latin was the language of learning during the Middle Ages. More scholars could now study these works for themselves. Among the most notable Greeks were Aristotle, who wrote on politics, animals, and physics; Hippocrates on medicine; and Euclid and Pythagoras on mathematics and geometry.

The Church was sometimes uneasy about the study of these writers, since their views often directly clashed with those of the Church. It feared that study of this kind might lead people to question the teachings of the Church, and possibly lose faith in its power to direct their lives.

PHILOSOPHY

Many famous philosophers lived during the Middle Ages. These men tried to find ways of explaining the meaning of life and the world. Men like Anselm of Aosta, in Italy, and Peter Abelard from France looked at philosophy from a Christian point of view. Anselm wrote a book called the *Proslogion* setting out to prove that God exists. He was eager to deepen his religious faith by finding rational arguments for religious beliefs. Although, like Anselm, Abelard was a sincere Christian, his work was condemned by the Church in 1141. As scholars began to rely on their own judgement rather than the teaching of the Church, such clashes of opinion became more common.

Part of a page from a Bible. Many medieval thinkers were interested in the study of God and the Bible. The Christian religion was the starting point of all their work.

An astronomer and his assistant. The study of stars interested many learned people, but not for wholly scientific reasons. The stars were thought to control people's fate.

ARITHMETIC

The study of arithmetic had always been important to the Church. Complicated calculations were done to work out the date of Easter each year. In the tenth century a scholar named Gerbert of Rheims began to use a calculating board known as an abacus. This was made up of balls strung along wires and held together in a frame. In the twelfth century the Arabic numerals which we still use today were introduced to western Europe, simplifying the process of calculation. Now it was more straightforward for merchants and others to draw up accounts showing the state of their finances.

THE SCIENCES

Science was thought of as part of philosophy. Many of those who wrote on scientific subjects, like the Englishmen Robert Grosseteste and Roger Bacon, were churchmen. Their religion deeply influenced their attitude toward knowledge, and they were greatly respected scholars.

A money-changer at work. On his bench, an abacus is marked out. This was used to make calculations, such as adding and subtracting.

29

The cover of a medieval book. Books were very costly to produce at this time. Text and illustrations were drawn by hand, often using expensive materials. It was quite usual for the covers of books to be studded with jewels.

Two cathedrals, one built in the Romanesque style, on the left, and the other in the Gothic style. Gothic architecture featured pointed arches, large areas of window, and, as in this example, many statues flanking the doorway. The Romanesque style was simpler.

In the Middle Ages much artistic work was carried out for the Church. Education too was mostly concerned with Church needs. As time went by, art and education began to develop in ways that were not involved with Church requirements.

NEW IDEAS ABOUT ART

The work of artists after the fall of the Roman Empire was very different from the work of earlier artists. Among tribes such as the Goths, Vandals, and Saxons, complex patterns that wove together animals, birds, and dragons were very popular. Patterns like these were also used by the early Christian artists of England and Ireland in the seventh and eighth centuries.

ART AND THE CHURCH

In the Middle Ages most art was made for a religious purpose. For instance, paintings and sculptures of Christ and the saints were made for churches to help people in their religious worship. Church services required special vessels, such as chalices for Mass, and these were often richly decorated. The furnishings of many churches were elaborate, intended

A page of the Lindisfarne Gospels. This famous illuminated manuscript was produced by the patient work of monks in the seventh century.

to show that those who planned and created them believed that no cost or effort was too great in the service of God. The abbey of Saint-Denis in France is one example. In the twelfth century much money was lavished on this abbey by its Abbot, Suger. Suger wrote an account describing how he hoped that those who saw the abbey's stained glass windows and jewels would think of the glory of God.

ARCHITECTURE

The style of architecture common in most of western Europe in the eleventh and twelfth centuries is known as "Romanesque." The buildings in this style were massive and imposing. The weight of their heavy stone roofs was carried by enormous pillars and round-headed arches. The Norman cathedral at Durham, England, is a classic example of this style of architecture.

A new style, known as "Gothic" architecture, began to develop in northern France in the twelfth century. The elegant Gothic style, with its pointed arches and delicate carvings, high walls and wide windows, quickly became very popular. Many great cathedrals were built in this style.

EDUCATION

In the Middle Ages education was mainly a privilege for men destined to follow a career in the Church. Some rulers were keen to improve education. King Alfred of Wessex and the Emperor Charlemagne were among these. But not all their plans to encourage education were successful, and it was not until the thirteenth century that education was available to a wider selection of people.

Schools were found in many monasteries and cathedrals. Universities were to develop out of some of the most important of these schools. Classes were in Latin, the teachers were priests or monks, and examinations were by spoken debate. In some countries, such as Italy, schools were established that did not concentrate on religious teaching alone. Subjects like arithmetic, which was useful to those taking up a life of trade, were taught.

BOOKS

The Church required books for its services. The printing press was not invented in western Europe until the fifteenth century, so all books had to be copied out by hand. The monasteries played an important role in the production of books. Monks made copies of manuscripts in part of the monastery called the "scriptorium." Here they produced Bibles and books of prayer. Many of these passed from one monastery to another, often from one country to another. Anselm of Aosta, in Italy, for example, sent copies of prayers to Gundolf, a monk of the abbey of Bec, in France. The manuscripts produced were very often "illuminated" (beautifully decorated) with pictures.

Early in the Middle Ages only members of the clergy had an education enabling them to read and write. However, by the thirteenth century, books were sometimes produced by lay people. Some of these were professional scribes, who copied out manuscripts to earn their living.

A scene at the royal court: the king is presented with a book. Many writers dedicated their work to important nobles. The poet Chaucer knew many people at the royal court in England, and dedicated many books to them.

Children at school, being taught by a monk. Few schools existed at this time, and education was very rare. Books were few, so children had to share.

The relics of saints were collected in many monasteries. They were kept in elaborate containers like this, known as reliquaries. Gold and precious stones were often used to decorate them.

Monasteries were built to house communities of monks or nuns who wanted to serve God and live together. Their way of life began in the third and fourth centuries, and gradually changed over a long period of time.

ST. BENEDICT

St. Benedict lived as a monk in Italy at the end of the fifth century. He founded many monasteries, including one at Monte Cassino near Naples, and wrote a book, *The Rule of St. Benedict*, that was a set of instructions for the monks' way of life. He suggested that the monks of each monastery should live together as a big family and obey the orders of their abbot. They were not to marry or have personal belongings. Each day was divided up so that the monks would spend a certain amount of time praying, working, and studying the Bible. St. Benedict's *"Rule"* became very popular, and many monasteries in the Middle Ages used it as their guide. Famous Benedictine monasteries included Bury St. Edmunds in Suffolk, England, and Cluny in Burgundy, part of modern France.

A pilgrim on his way to pray at the tomb of St. Thomas Becket in Canterbury. Pilgrims flocked to pray at monasteries that claimed to house the relics of saints. This picture is from an edition of the Canterbury Tales *by Chaucer.*

LIFE IN THE MONASTERY

In the Middle Ages monasteries were among the most important centers of learning, and monks were some of the most learned people of the time. Schools were often set up in monasteries. The monks made copies of the Bible and many works of scholarship, writing them out by hand and decorating them with a number of magnificent illustrations.

During the medieval period, life in many monasteries changed. The first monks tried not to be involved in the everyday life of the people of the towns and villages around the monastery. But this was not easy. Many monasteries became rich and powerful, often because of gifts of land or money given by people who wanted the monks and nuns to pray for them. This often led to dishonesty and corruption in the Church, and many people began to attack the monks' way of life. Their abbots often became important figures in society. They were visited by kings, queens, and nobles, and were expected to provide hospitality for their guests. When King Edward I of England visited Lanercost Priory in 1306, he took almost 200 servants and soldiers with him. All these people had to be housed and fed in the monastery!

The monastery church was the central part of a monk's life, because prayers were the most important part of every day. Many people asked to be remembered in these prayers.

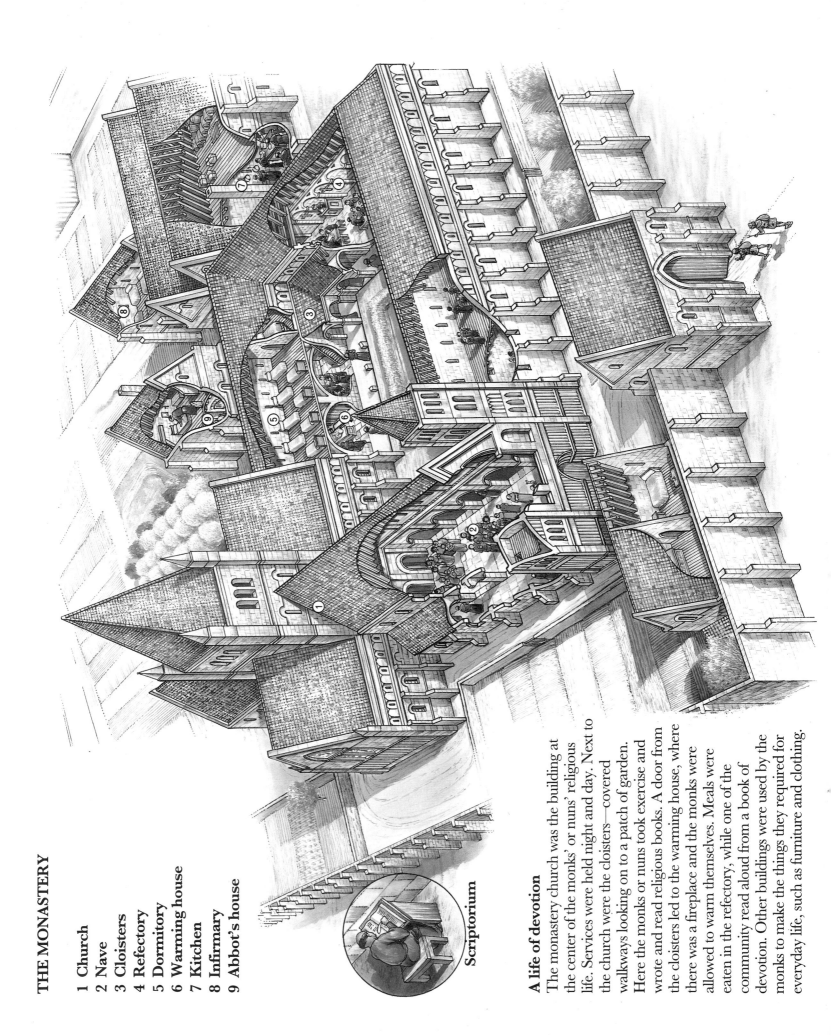

THE MONASTERY

1 Church
2 Nave
3 Cloisters
4 Refectory
5 Dormitory
6 Warming house
7 Kitchen
8 Infirmary
9 Abbot's house

Scriptorium

A life of devotion

The monastery church was the building at the center of the monks' or nuns' religious life. Services were held night and day. Next to the church were the cloisters—covered walkways looking on to a patch of garden. Here the monks or nuns took exercise and wrote and read religious books. A door from the cloisters led to the warming house, where there was a fireplace and the monks were allowed to warm themselves. Meals were eaten in the refectory, while one of the community read aloud from a book of devotion. Other buildings were used by the monks to make the things they required for everyday life, such as furniture and clothing.

A monk writing. Friars became popular because they went out and worked among the people, especially in towns, unlike the monks who were supposed to remain shut away in their monasteries.

Flagellants were people who whipped themselves as a form of public penance for the sins of the world. They hoped that their actions would persuade God to bring times of health and peace, rather than the suffering caused by the Black Death.

The Franciscan and Dominican orders of friars were founded in the thirteenth century. Their work was very different from that of the monks, who went to isolated places to spend their time in prayer. The friars were anxious to work in the community, preaching and helping the sick.

ST. FRANCIS OF ASSISI

St. Francis was born in the Italian town of Assisi in 1182, the son of a prosperous cloth merchant. He spent his time in prayer, inspired by Christ and his Apostles, and gave up all his possessions. He lived a life of simplicity, in contrast to the wealth and apparent corruption of the Church, and became popular, especially with the poor. In time other people came to him, wanting to share this life of absolute poverty and religion. St. Francis and his followers had no permanent home. They wandered from town to town, teaching those whom they met about God, begging for food and shelter when they needed it.

The pope, Innocent III, gave his permission for Francis and his followers to go about their work. Francis' followers were known as Franciscans, or "Gray" friars. They were given this name because of the gray habits they wore.

ST. DOMINIC

St. Dominic was born in Castile, and his story was very different from that of St. Francis. Dominic came from a noble family. He became a priest and was sent to Provence at the beginning of the thirteenth century to help convert heretics. At this time Dominic became very aware of how important it was to provide education for the clergy. Many parish priests were poorly educated and unable to teach the people in their care. Like Francis, Dominic attracted a band of supporters who shared his views. They lived a life of poverty and worked in the towns. Because they wore black habits, they were known as "Black" friars. The Dominicans produced many famous scholars, including St. Thomas Aquinas, Roger Bacon, Duns Scotus, and William of Ockham.

ST. CLARE

Many women were eager to take up this new way of religious life. Their leader, St. Clare, asked St. Francis to draw up a rule of life for them to follow. They too lived a life of poverty, but, unlike the friars, they lived in permanent buildings and did not go out into the world. St. Clare's followers were known as "Minoresses."

THE WORK OF THE FRIARS

Some friars worked with sick people, others were teachers, but one of their most important tasks was to preach. All over Europe parish priests complained that people flocked to listen to the friars rather than going to the regular services of the Church.

The friars were also involved in missionary work. In the fourteenth century one Franciscan, an Italian named John of Monte Corvino, traveled to Peking to try to convert the Chinese to Christianity.

FRIARS AND HERESY

Religious beliefs of which the Church did not approve were labeled heresies. Many heresies grew up in Europe from the eleventh century onward. In the Netherlands the teaching of the heretic Lambert le Bègue became popular. In England the Lollard heresy gained many supporters. The Cathar heresy was strong in Italy and France. Heresies like these often challenged the position of priests and the importance of particular services and beliefs, such as Mass. Leaders of the Church felt threatened by them. Heretics who refused to give up their beliefs could be tortured or executed.

POLITICS AND HERESY

Sometimes people were accused of heresy for political reasons. This happened to a French girl named Joan of Arc. Joan helped to lead her country against the English during the Hundred Years War. The English captured her and accused her of witchcraft, and Joan was burned at the stake as a heretic in 1431. Not long afterward her case was looked at again, and she was declared innocent of all charges. In 1920 she was made a saint.

A picture painted by the famous Italian painter Giotto. It shows St. Francis, founder of the Franciscan friars. The birds around him show his gentleness, humility, and love of creation.

A friar preaching. The friars became well known for their preaching and teaching work among people in towns and villages. Many people came to hear them.

During the Middle Ages trade gradually increased, and towns began to flourish. A wide variety of tradesmen practiced in the towns, from tailors to cobblers, bankers to cloth merchants.

TOWN LIFE
Life in a town was noisy, busy, and dirty. The streets were narrow and crowded with people on their way to the shops and markets. Pickpockets and cutpurses were always on the lookout for unsuspecting travelers with coins in their purses. The town was a place where crime flourished. The layout of medieval towns can sometimes still be seen. Bury St. Edmunds in Suffolk, England, is one example.

A NEW BEGINNING
Significant changes in the economy began to take place from the eleventh century. Some towns grew rich because specialized industries developed in them. The woolen industry in the towns of Flanders is a good example of this. A number of cities such as Venice and Genoa in Italy were involved in long-distance trade. One of the most famous of the merchants of Venice was Marco Polo, who traveled to the Mongol Empire in the East in the thirteenth century. There were also towns that prospered for religious reasons. A town with the shrine of a famous saint might attract many pilgrims who would bring gifts and money to the area.

A map of the world drawn in the thirteenth century. During the Middle Ages much of the world was unknown territory to the people of Europe, and it was believed that the entire world was made up of three continents: Europe, Africa, and Asia.

THE SEARCH FOR TRADE

At the beginning of the Middle Ages most trade was in luxury goods but soon there was trade in everyday items, like foodstuffs, as well as luxuries. The city of Genoa played a great part in trade. It produced little food itself and was eager to look for other countries that would provide it with grain. Genoese merchants were also involved in the search for trading opportunities far from home. There was much trade with Byzantium and the East. Genoese merchants bought honey, nuts, wine, carpets, alum, and spices from countries farther east, and sold them in the West.

POPULATION GROWTH

The population of Europe grew steadily at this time. Because the number of births, marriages, and deaths were not recorded during the Middle Ages, it is difficult to find exact figures. One famous historian believes that the population of France rose from about 2.5 million in the middle of the thirteenth century to 13.5 million in the middle of the fourteenth century! This seems like such a large increase that some historians think the figures must be wrong. But it seems very clear that great growth had taken place all over Europe.

Many people left the countryside to start a new life in the towns, and this meant that the town population grew. Houses were often very small, and streets very narrow. Drains were open, and rubbish and sewage littered the streets. Town life was often unhygienic, unpleasant, and dangerous.

Trade was mainly carried out by sea in the Middle Ages. This picture shows ships and merchants in port.

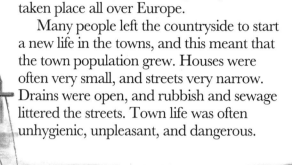

FAMOUS TOWNS

The towns in Italy and Flanders were among the most famous of the Middle Ages. They led the way in trade and commerce. Banking and accounting developed in Italy to help merchants trade more easily. The Florentine banking firms of Bardi and Peruzzi were well known in many different countries of Europe.

The merchants of a number of German cities banded together to form trading associations. They shipped fish, timber, tar, grain, and other commodities from the Baltic to countries like Flanders and England. Cities like these earned a reputation for their power and wealth.

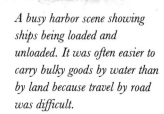

A busy harbor scene showing ships being loaded and unloaded. It was often easier to carry bulky goods by water than by land because travel by road was difficult.

INDUSTRY

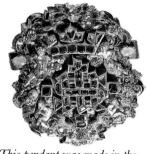

This pendant was made in the fifteenth century in Germany. Luxury goods like this were produced by highly skilled craftsmen.

Craftsmen at work making glass. Glass was produced by blending sand and potash together in a furnace heated to a high temperature. The liquid glass was then taken at the end of a long hollow pipe to be blown into shape.

Industry in the Middle Ages operated on a small scale, because most of the population were still working on the land. Most goods were manufactured by hand. Gradually larger-scale organization developed and some mechanical power was used. The woolen industry was one of the first to take advantage of these new developments.

THE WOOLEN INDUSTRY

When woolen cloth was made to be sold, the process was highly organized. Many craftspeople were involved in the process. Some worked in their own homes, where the wool or cloth was brought to them by a merchant. Others were employed in the town workshops. The wool was first spun to make thread, often by women known as "spinsters." The thread was taken to a weaver who wove it into cloth using a loom, which he worked with his hands and feet.

Fulling and dyeing woolen cloth. These cloth-making processes were carried out without mechanical power until fulling mills gradually came into use.

The cloth was now ready for "fulling," which involved soaking the cloth and beating it until it became thicker. At first this was done by a "fuller" who trampled the cloth underfoot in water. Because of this, fullers were occasionally called "walkers." These names sometimes stuck and became surnames. After the fulling process, the cloth was stretched, dried, brushed, and trimmed. The dyer was the next craftsman to work on the cloth. Dyeing was carried out in a large vat.

The most important change in the cloth industry during this period was the use of water power. From about the twelfth century, water-powered mills were built for use in the fulling process. Now cloth was fulled by mechanical- and water-power. Swiftly flowing streams were needed to power the fulling mills, so from this time on the cloth industry was often based in the countryside.

WORKING WITH GLASS

Glass was rare and expensive. The art of creating colored glass windows, showing magnificent pictures, flourished from the tenth century onward. The colors were made by adding metals like copper and iron oxides to the glass. Glass of this kind was used in many great churches. Examples can still be seen at the cathedrals of Poitiers and Chartres in France. Here nearly 200 medieval windows survive. The purples, deep blues, greens, and reds of these windows are especially famous.

WORKING WITH PRECIOUS STONES

Precious stones were worn as jewelry by important people. Rich men and women wore rings. The jewelry of Arnegunde, Queen of the Franks, was discovered by archaeologists, and tells us a lot about the work of medieval jewelers. It included round gold brooches set with garnets, earrings, and a gold ring inscribed with her name. Jewels were also used to beautify churches. They were used for statues of saints and for reliquaries (the cases in which relics were kept).

A medieval window from the Gothic cathedral of Notre Dame in Paris. Stained glass was produced by adding metals to the glass in a liquid state. Beautiful colors and designs were formed, and these windows made a grand, colorful spectacle in churches and cathedrals.

OTHER TEXTILES

Other textiles used at this time included linen, velvet, and silk. Only the rich could afford to buy velvet and silk. Velvet was first made in Europe in the thirteenth century. Silk was brought to Europe from the East, but from the twelfth century Italy became known for the manufacture of silk. In Venice and Florence there were especially skilled silk-workers.

WORKING WITH METALS

Mining was carried out in the Middle Ages. Iron ore was mined in places like Germany and England, but the process was dangerous and difficult. Removing the soil, providing air for the miners, and pumping out water were all very hard work without the sophisticated technology we have today.

One very important use of metal was in the making of armor. The work of the armorers of Germany and northern Italy was in great demand. Metal could also be used for tools, which were used by craftsmen to produce everyday items.

Towns were crowded and dirty. People often lived above their shops, and buildings were tall and narrow, many packed into one street. The buildings were made of wattle and daub and timber. This, plus the overcrowding, made the streets a real fire and disease risk.

Medieval transport was uncomfortable. Here a horse-drawn wagon takes two people to market in town.

THE WORK OF THE GUILDS

Life in a town was mostly ruled by guilds of merchants and craftsmen. Guilds were organizations that controlled much of the business life of the time. The masters of each guild supervised wages, prices, and the quality of work done by guild members. The range of guilds was very wide, from saddle-makers to fullers, weavers, and bakers.

The guilds had such power that only their members were allowed to trade and work in the various crafts. The most senior members of a guild were the masters. Masters had their own shops, where they worked with their staff. The workers included journeymen, who were paid a daily wage, and apprentices (boys or girls who were being trained as craftspeople). Guilds were also concerned with the welfare of their members. They collected money to give to those who were sick or too old to work.

MERCHANTS

Merchants dominated the town's business life, and were also members of the council that ruled over the town. In the city of Florence prosperous merchants and guilds held political power. Here the important political positions were held almost totally by cloth merchants.

HOLIDAYS IN TOWN

Work stopped on special religious feast days, and there were celebrations when important visitors entered the town, or when a marriage took place in a great local family.

At times like these, there was an atmosphere of carnival in town. Guild members would parade through the streets, dressed in special costumes, and carrying their own distinctive banners. Stories from the Bible were acted out. These were known as "mystery" plays. The guilds would act out a story appropriate to their trade. Fishmongers often chose the story of Jonah and the whale, for example. Townspeople enjoyed many different entertainments—from horse racing, cock-fighting, wrestling, skating, and soccer, to eating and drinking in cook and wine shops.

These three people are bakers, at work in the town. Work stopped for religious festivals. These were celebrated with processions and fairs, which gave busy tradesmen like these a chance to relax.

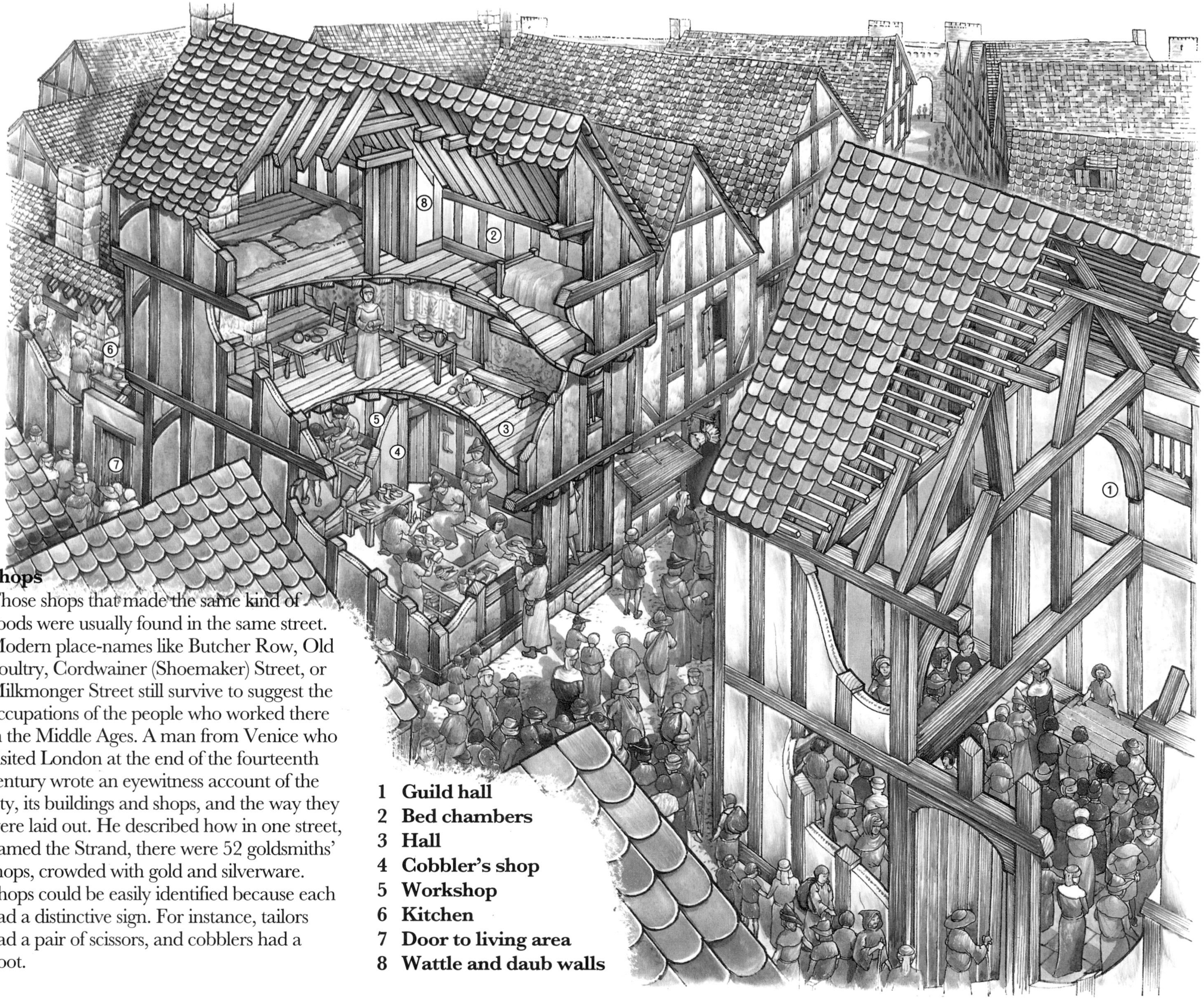

Shops

Those shops that made the same kind of goods were usually found in the same street. Modern place-names like Butcher Row, Old Poultry, Cordwainer (Shoemaker) Street, or Milkmonger Street still survive to suggest the occupations of the people who worked there in the Middle Ages. A man from Venice who visited London at the end of the fourteenth century wrote an eyewitness account of the city, its buildings and shops, and the way they were laid out. He described how in one street, named the Strand, there were 52 goldsmiths' shops, crowded with gold and silverware. Shops could be easily identified because each had a distinctive sign. For instance, tailors had a pair of scissors, and cobblers had a boot.

1 Guild hall
2 Bed chambers
3 Hall
4 Cobbler's shop
5 Workshop
6 Kitchen
7 Door to living area
8 Wattle and daub walls

I llness was common in medieval Europe, where the spread of diseases like the plague killed thousands of people. Medical practices developed slowly over the course of the Middle Ages.

DISEASE

Disease was a part of everyday life. Many illnesses existed for which there was no treatment, and sufferers accepted that they simply had to live with them. Leprosy, an infectious skin disease, was one such illness. Lepers were ordered to live by themselves because of the risk of infection, and sometimes laws were passed to prevent them from entering towns. This happened in Paris at the end of the fifteenth century. In some places, houses were built where lepers could live together, usually well away from the town. In the thirteenth century there were seven leper houses near the French town of Toulouse alone. Lepers were greatly feared, and many people who had skin complaints were also treated as if they had leprosy. Other common diseases for which there was no cure at this time were measles, tuberculosis, dysentery, diptheria, smallpox, and scarlet fever.

Mixing and selling drugs, medieval-style. Much of the medical wisdom of the ancient worlds of Greece and Rome was lost during the Middle Ages. Medical treatment was often based on guesswork, and people often found comfort in herbal treatments.

A medieval painting showing a miracle, as people who are ill touch the cloak of a saint and are cured. Many people thought that religious belief could bring about cures like this.

A doctor treating a patient. During the Middle Ages, there were few hospitals, so most patients were treated in their own homes.

One day the rags of a beggar who had died of plague were thrown into the street. Two pigs tore at the clothing. They fell dead at once, as if they had been poisoned.

Boccaccio

PLAGUE

The most feared of all diseases was bubonic plague, known as the Black Death. It was brought to Europe along trade routes from the East, and broke out first in Italy in 1347. From here it spread quickly into many countries. As thousands died, panic erupted. Between 20 and 40 percent of the population was killed. Bubonic plague was carried by rats and fleas. Its symptoms were lumps in the armpits and on other parts of the body.

Some Italian cities tried to set up a system of quarantine. Visitors wanting to enter the city had to wait nearby for a certain period of time before they were given permission to enter. The cities hoped that during this time, they would be able to see who was sick and who was healthy.

MEDICINE

Medical treatment was a combination of prayer, traditional folk beliefs, experiments based on observing patients who were ill, and knowledge handed down from the ancient worlds of Greece and Rome.

An English poet named Chaucer, who lived in the fourteenth century, described how people tried to treat illness—both in people and in animals—by using magic charms. This was a very common custom in all parts of Europe. Chaucer also explained how many people believed that a person's character and health were determined by a mixture of elements known as "humors": blood, phlegm, yellow bile, and black bile. The humors were made of a combination of four elements: fire, water, air, and earth. Doctors would advise their patients to eat foods that were suited to people with a particular sort of humor.

An important development at this time was the study of the human body. Dissections were carried out at universities such as Bologna, in Italy. The number of dissections grew considerably from the fourteenth century, and led to a greater general understanding of how the body worked.

KEEPING CLEAN

One reason why plague spread rapidly in the towns was because of unhygienic conditions. It was not until the nineteenth century that doctors and nurses fully realized the importance of cleanliness in good health. In the Middle Ages many people lived in a very dirty environment. Rubbish, human dung, and other matter from shops and houses was thrown into the streets and left to rot.

An outbreak of plague in a medieval town. Writers such as Boccaccio described the feeling of terror when plague broke out. Whole families could be killed by the plague.

43

THE MIDDLE AGES END

The use of guns and cannons, like the one above, meant that the way wars were fought changed dramatically during the Middle Ages. Machines came to dominate battles, rather than knights on horseback.

Slowly, many changes took place in the Middle Ages. The feudal system, the Church's influence on daily life, and the structure of society all began to change. New ideas developed to take their place.

THE CHURCH

During much of the Middle Ages the Church influenced many different parts of people's lives. But the Church came in for increasing criticism. The idea of the pope having political power was challenged by the rulers of different European countries. Thinkers, like the Italian poet Dante (1265–1321), who turned their attention to questions of politics, were very much opposed to the Church's claims to political power.

In the fourteenth and fifteenth centuries criticism of the Church came to a head. Many people lost respect for popes who seemed too involved in politics.

Ego sum Papa.

In the later Middle Ages many people began to attack what they saw as faults in the Church, such as greed and corruption. This picture is criticizing the pope by showing him as a devil.

A page from the Bible, produced using a printing press in the early 1450s. Toward the end of the Middle Ages, the Bible was translated from Latin into many European languages. People could now read the Bible for themselves, rather than having its meaning explained by priests. This represented a great change.

DISAGREEMENT AND DEBATE

A period of disagreement about who should be pope followed. The dispute is known as the Great Schism. A series of rival popes was elected, and each pope had his party of followers. Many people lost their faith in the Church at this time.

Ordinary people turned against other members of the clergy, such as badly educated priests, and also monks and nuns who did not keep their religious vows. All these things meant that the Catholic Church had less control over people's lives. People began to demand the right to think for themselves about education, politics, and religion, instead of accepting the teachings of the Church.

WARFARE

Warfare also began to change at this time. Knights had always been the most important part of any medieval army, and the nobility spent much time training for war. The use of gunpowder and the development of artillery transformed the way battles were fought. Gunpowder was known in China as early as the eleventh century, but it was not until the thirteenth century that a western European writer gave an account of how to make gunpowder. Guns and cannons developed after this. The use of weapons like these meant that castles and fortified towns became much less secure. The old ideals of knighthood died away and the nobility devoted their lives to politics and elegant living rather than simply warfare.

COUNTRY AND TOWN

During the Middle Ages most of the population of Europe lived in the country. The standard of living depended on local agriculture. For the poorest people, the question was whether their land would produce enough for them to eat at all. For knights and noblemen, agriculture provided income from rents and sales of farm produce. As time went on, more people came to rely on a way of life that was not based in the country, but in the growing towns. Although agriculture was still extremely important, trade and manufacturing began to provide work for many more people—and for some they also provided wealth.

A NEW KIND OF WORLD

The Middle Ages ended in about the fifteenth century. Changes in the way people thought about religion, and developments in warfare and in the economy, had gradually led to a new kind of society. There was great belief in people's power to change and control every aspect of their lives. People in medieval times would not have believed this to be possible. As ideas like these became strong, the medieval world vanished, and a new kind of world arrived.

A printing press at work producing books. During the Middle Ages all books were copied by hand. The printing press, which came into use in the fifteenth century, altered the process completely.

KEY DATES AND GLOSSARY

410	City of Rome sacked by Alaric the Bold and Visigoths
442	Roman troops leave Britain
476	Last Roman emperor in the West overthrown
496	Clovis, king of the Franks, adopts Christianity
800	Coronation of the Emperor Charlemagne
c.800	Start of Viking raids in Europe. These lasted into the tenth century
c.1000–1150	Romanesque architecture popular in Europe
c.1050	Beginnings of universities in Europe
1066	Norman conquest of England. William of Normandy becomes king of England
1071	Seljuk Turks defeat the Greek emperors of Byzantium
1086	*Domesday Book* completed
1095	Council of Clermont, where Urban II preaches the First Crusade
1096–99	First Crusade. Crusaders capture Jerusalem from the Muslims
1098	Beginnings of Cistercian movement to reform monastic life
c.1100	Revival of interest in the classical work of Greece and Rome and introduction of Arabic science to Europe
1147–49	Second Crusade organized by St. Bernard of Clairvaux. Crusaders try to take Damascus and fail
1187	Jerusalem captured by Muslims
1189–92	Third Crusade led by Frederick Barbarossa of Germany, Richard I of England, and Philip Augustus of France. Richard I reaches truce with Muslim leader, Saladin
c.1200	Gothic art and architecture popular in Europe
1204	Fourth Crusade called by Pope Innocent III. Constantinople attacked by Crusaders and Latin Empire set up
1212	Children's Crusade
1215	Great Charter of Liberties granted by King John of England to his subjects (Magna Carta)
c.1275	Marco Polo arrives at the court of Kublai Khan, the Mongol Emperor of China and Mongolia
1291	Acre, last Christian stronghold in the Holy Land, conquered by Muslims
1307	Death of King Edward I of England, under whom Parliament began to become important
1337	Beginning of Hundred Years War between England and France

c.1340–1400 Life of Chaucer, the English
        poet
1347–49 Black Death
1378–1417 Great Schism in Church
1381   Peasants' Revolt in England
1412-31 Life of Joan of Arc
1415   Battle of Agincourt
c.1450   Invention of printing press with
        movable type
1453   Constantinople overthrown by the
        Turks
1485   Death of Richard III of England at
        Battle of Bosworth

Glossary

archaeology: the study of the past by scientific analysis of material remains and objects rather than written records

Bayeux Tapestry: an embroidery made to commemorate the Norman victory at the Battle of Hastings in 1066

Black Death: the plague

Crusade: a holy war fought by Christians for their religion

cutpurse: a thief who steals by cutting people's purses from them

Domesday Book: a record of people who held land in England under King William I

famine: a time of food shortage when people starve

feudalism: a term used by historians to describe the way that medieval society was organized

fief: an area of land held by a lord

guild: a society of merchants or traders

heretic: someone who argues with the teachings of the Church

Holy Land: an area of the Middle East described in the Bible

illuminated manuscripts: handwritten, brightly illustrated books and documents

knight: an important medieval soldier

manor: the area of land in the countryside owned and run by the lord

pagans: people who were not Christians, and worshipped gods like the Sun

philosophy: the study of how people think and how the world works

pilgrim: someone who journeys to a sacred place to pray

relic: the material remains of a saint—e.g. bones or clothing

reliquary: the case in which relics are kept

siege engine: a machine such as a large catapult, used to attack a town or castle

squire: a boy who served a knight

tournament: a competition held between two or more knights

villein: a peasant

wattle and daub: mixture of straw, sticks, mud, and clay used for building

The quotations

Latin was the language of the Church and of education in the Middle Ages, and so the majority of documents at this time were written in Latin. Most of the quotations in this book have been translated from Latin.

INDEX

Page numbers in italics refer to captions

Abacus 29, *29*
agriculture 16, *16*, *18*, 19, 45
Alfred of Wessex 31
Anselm of Aosta 29, 31
arithmetic 29, 31
astrolabe *28*
Augustine, St. 28

Banquet 14, *15*
baptism 6, 8
Barbarossa, Frederick 27
Bayeux Tapestry *4*, 5, 10
Bede 6
beekeeping *18*
Benedict, St. 32
Benedictines 11, 32
bestiary *28*
Bible 28, *29*, 31, 32, *33*
Black Death *34*, 42
Boccaccio 42, *43*
books *30*, 31, *31*
bubonic plague 42

Castles 7, *9*, 15, 22, 23, 24, *25*
cathedrals 7, *7*, 31, 39
Charlemagne, Emperor 6, 10, 11, 18, 31
Chaucer *3*, 28, *32*, 43
Children's Crusade 26, 27
chivalry 20, 21
Chrétien de Troyes 21
Christianity 4, 26
Cistercians 11, 15
Clare, St. 35
coat of arms *10*, 22
Constantine, Emperor 6
Crusades, the 26, *26*, 27

Disease 42
doctors 42, *42*, 43
Domesday Book 16
Dominic, St. 34
Dominicans 34

Education 8, *22*, 30, 31, 44
Edward I 32

Famine 7, 14
feasts 14, 15
feudal society 5
flagellants *34*
Francis of Assisi, St. 34, 35, *35*
Franciscans 34
friars 34, *34*, 35, *35*
fulling mills 16, 38, *38*

Germanic tribes 4, *5*, 6
glass *38*, 39, *39*
Gothic architecture 30, *30*
Gottfried von Strasburg 9
Great Schism 44
Greek writers 28, 43
guilds 40

Hagia Sophia *6*
Harold of Wessex *4*, 5
heresy 35
Holy Land 26, 27
Hundred Years War, the 18, 23, 35
hunting 9, 10, 12, 13, *13*, 14, 23, *23*

Innocent III, Pope 34

Jerusalem 11, 26, *26*, 27
jesters 9, *12*
jewelry *38*, 39
Joan of Arc 35
Jocelin of Brakelond 16

Kings 6, *9*, *12*, 13, 18, 22, 23, 24, *31*, 32
King Arthur 21
knights 7, 8, 9, 10, 12, *12*, 13, 20, *20*, 21, *21*, 22, 23, 24, 26, 27, 45
Krak des Chevaliers 23, *27*

Labor services 18, 19
leprosy 42
lords 5, 8, *11*, 12, 16, 18, 19, 24, 25

Map, Walter 22
Marco Polo 36
marriage 8, *8*, 9
medicine 42, *42*, 43
merchants 36, 37, *37*, 40
mills 16

mining 39
monasteries 7, 19, 31, 32, *33*
monks 11, *11*, 15, 31, *31*, 32, *33*, 34
motte and bailey castles 24, *24*

Nobles 7, 10, 11, 13, 22, *22*, 23, 25, 32, 45
nuns 11, 15, 32, 33

Paper mills 16
peasants 8, *8*, 9, 10, 12, 14, 18, 19, 26
Peasants' Revolt 19
Peter the Hermit 27
philosophy 29
pilgrimage 11, *32*
plague 42, 43, *43*
population 37
printing press 31, *45*
Proslogion 29

Reliquary *32*, 39
Richard I 27, *27*
Roman Empire 4, *5*, 18
Romanesque architecture 30, *30*
Ruthwell Cross *6*

Saladin 27, *27*
scriptorium 31
seal *22*
shield *10*
shops *41*
siege engines 24
spinning 10, *10*, 38
squire 20, *21*
Suger, Abbot 30
sumptuary laws 11
swords *20*, 21

Tapestry 23, *24*
tournaments 12, *12*, 13, 23

Urban II, Pope 26

Vikings *4*

Water mills 16, *17*, 38
William of Normandy *4*, 5
windmills 16
woolen industry 36, 38, *38*, *39*

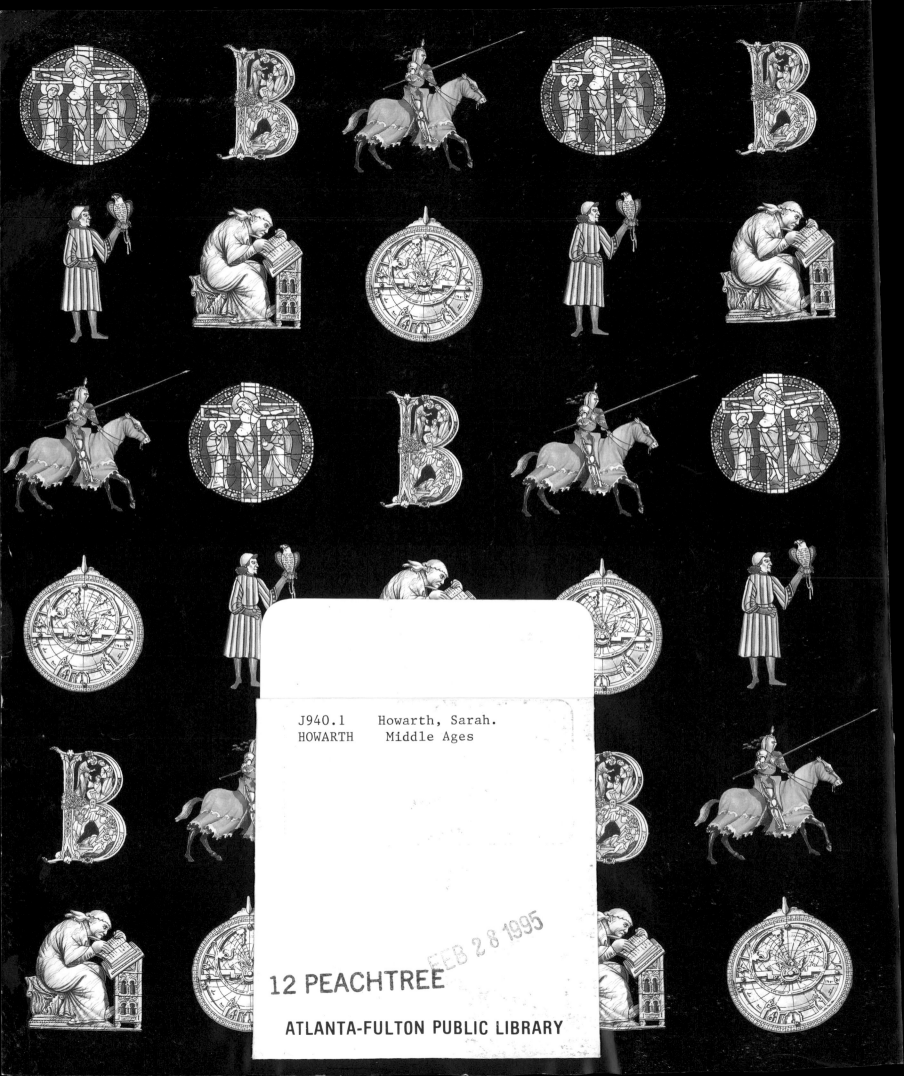